Island of Flowers

A Seasonal Guide to Wild Flowers of the Wight

To Pat & Phil,
With best wishes
from Judith.

Island of Flowers

A Seasonal Guide to Wild Flowers of the Wight

Illustrations and Text by
Judith Hammer

AMPERSAND

First published in 2008
by Ampersand
Hill Place, Thorley, Yarmouth
Isle of Wight PO41 0XJ

ISBN 978-0-9556354-1-0

Design and typesetting by Ampersand

Printed on 75 per cent recycled paper
and 25 per cent from sustainable resource
by Crossprint, Newport, Isle of Wight

Contents

Foreword

by Alan Titchmarsh MBE VMH DL

Since I can remember I have gone on country walks with my eyes on the ground. It was something that Baden Powell deplored in his *Scouting for Boys*, exhorting the youth of the early twentieth century to stride out with their heads held high. But as a boy who was passionate about nature and wild flowers, it was on the ground that my interest lay. The rewards have ben rich; I have come to love our native flowers more than any exotic species. They have, for the most part, a subtle charm, and occasionally rise to spectacle: a hedge bank awash with Queen Anne's lace in April, or a cliff top carpeted with thrift in May. But whatever they look like, they are *our* wild flowers, part of *our* landscape, *our* everyday life and deserve to be cherished and celebrated. The Isle of Wight offers floral delights far greater than its size would lead you to believe, so for me botanizing trips here are especially rewarding.

For many years I have prized Revd W. Keble Martin's *Concise British Flora* for its information and for the beautiful flower portraits it contains. Now I can add to my shelves Judith Hammer's fine flora of the Isle of Wight. When I first opened its covers I was astonished at its beauty. Many hours of painstaking artistry have gone into the creation of this wonderful book, which deserves to be on the bookshelf of every house on the Island. Not simply because it will prove to be useful – listing the Island habitats of the flowers so that you can go and acquaint yourself with them in person – but also because a labour of such love and dedication deserves recognition. Judith's flowers come to life on the page – a rare talent when it comes to botanical art. I envy her skill and salute her endeavours. This is one of the most charming books I have ever opened.

Alan Titchmarsh

Introduction

This is not an academic book, nor is it a complete collection of Island flowers. It is simply a personal gathering of some 200 flowers and fruits painted during 2006 and 2007. The latter year was a particularly good one for plants generally, and especially wild flowers. Whilst we were complaining about the rain and lack of summer weather, they were having a bonanza! The project is one that I have long had in mind but that I have only recently managed to tackle.

Originally I planned simply to make my own record of the wild flower year, but I was persuaded to share these studies with others by gathering them into a book. I hope that it will encourage readers to enjoy our lovely countryside even more as they look for flowers when out walking.

I have painted the flowers as I found them. They are not grouped in families, but *roughly* in order of flowering throughout the year. Of course, most flowers bloom for more than one month, and so the order is a little 'general'. I began with a Snowdrop and ended with the seedheads of Burdock – there is plenty in between!

The Island has gradually become more and more urbanised, and wild flowers have diminished. The roadside verges are constantly being cut, often just as the flower seeds are setting, and hedges have been grubbed out in many places. The headlands of fields have often been ploughed up and crops are widely sprayed. All this has reduced the habitat for wild flowers.

On the Island we have at least six completely different habitats for flowers in a very small area: hedges and banks, woodland, downs, rough grassland, damp places near streams, and the seashore. There is also a great variety of soil, ranging from clay and sand to chalk and peat. These factors contribute to the wonderful variety of flowers we have here. Most flowers are, of course, to be found also in other parts of the UK, but probably never in this variety in such close proximity.

I have suggested the most likely habitats for each flower, and in some instances I have mentioned where I myself have found it. As I live in Thorley, my references are especially orientated to the West Wight. However, for the most part I have generalised about location, as the majority of flowers can be found all over the Island.

For more detailed botanical information about specific plants there are a number of books available. I would recommend:

The Wild Flowers of Britain and Northern Europe : Fitter & Blamey (*Collins*) – an inexpensive paperback.

The Illustrated Flora of Britain and Northern Europe : Blamey & Grey-Wilson *(Hodder & Stoughton)* – a large format hardback.

The definitive academic book for Island flowers is The Isle of Wight Flora : Pope, Snow & Allen (*The Dovecote Press*) – now out of print, but available from libraries.

I am grateful for suggestions made by friends, especially Sue and Chris Reed who have also been kind enough to give their time to checking both text and illustrations.

Without an enormous amount of work done by my husband, Mark, this book would never have been undertaken. I owe him a huge debt of gratitude for his encouragement and all he has done in designing and typesetting the text, and preparing the book for publication.

Judith Hammer
Thorley
April 2008

Identification Key

There are, of course, several ways of identifying a wild flower: by colour, shape, size, habitat and season. Over the next pages I have broadly classified the flowers in this book according to their predominant colour, and within each colour range. I have tried to narrow the field even further by taking size and flower shape into account, though descriptions are inevitably approximate. However, I hope that by referring to this 'key' and then to individual pages you will find the process of identification both simpler and more rewarding.

Separate petals

Bell shaped

Round ball

Cone shaped

Cluster of tiny flowers

Small lipped trumpet

Pea flower

S small (up to 15cm) **M medium** (15–40cm) **T tall** (above 40cm) **Bush**

a PINK flower could be

– with separate petals

M Red Campion *[bright pink]* 22
S Herb Robert 24
S Hedgerow Cranesbill 30
M Flowering Rush 36
B Dog Rose 50
M Ragged Robin 48
T Marsh Mallow 64
T Rosebay Willowherb *[bright]* 78
M Broad-leaved Willowherb 84
M Musk Mallow 88
T Great Willowherb *[bright]* 90

– with lipped trumpets

S Red Dead-nettle *[pink]* 10
M Toothwort 30
M Common Fumitory 48
M Wild Basil 90

– with clusters of flowers

S Musk Storksbill 22
M Red Valerian 26
S Thrift 36
S/M Common Centaury 66
VS Squinancywort *[pale]* 66
T Hemp Agrimony 84

– with flowers in a ball

S Red Clover *[pink]* 52

– if cone shaped

S Field Bindweed *[convolvulus]* 54
M Sea Bindweed 60

– if spiked

S Redshank 68

– with pea flower

S Rest-harrow 74

a YELLOW flower could be

– with separate petals

S Primrose *[pale]* 10
S Lesser Celandine 10
M Meadow Buttercup 28
T Marsh Marigold 32
M Creeping Buttercup 34
T Yellow Iris 38
M Herb Bennet *[small petals]* 40
S Common Rock-rose 46
M Greater Spearwort 52
S/M Yellow-wort 54
M Yellow Horned-poppy 56
S Silverweed 70
M/T Agrimony 70
S Creeping Cinquefoil 72

– with 'dandelion-like' petals

S/M Dandelion 14
M Few-leaved Hawkweed 26
S Coltsfoot 32
S Golden Samphire 62
S/M Leafy Hawkweed 68
T Elecampane *[very large]* 72
S Common Fleabane 76
M Smooth Sow-thistle 86
M Prickly Sow-thistle 88
S/M Rough Hawkbit 92

– if bell shaped

S Cowslip 16

– with flowers in a ball

S Groundsel 14
S Black Meddick 26
M Hop Trefoil 90

– with clusters of flowers

M Lady's Bedstraw 68
M/T St John's Wort 74
M Wild Mignonette 84
M/T Ragwort 92

– with lipped trumpets

S/M Yellow Rattle 34
B Honeysuckle 58

- with pea flower

B Gorse 14
S/M Kidney Vetch 40
M Greater Birdsfoot Trefoil 42
S Birdsfoot Trefoil 66
S Common Toadflax 80
M Narrow-leaved Birdsfoot Trefoil 84

Miscellaneous

S Wild Daffodil 18
B Hazel Catkin 18

a CREAM flower could be

– with clusters of flowers

B Dogwood 40
B Elderflower 50
M Rock Samphire *[flat]* 62
T Meadowsweet 64

– with separate petals

S Field Pansy 16

a WHITE flower could be

– with separate petals

S Wood Anemone 14
Wild Cherry 16
B Blackthorn 18
S Greater Stitchwort 18
S Wild Strawberry 20
S Daisy *[many & small]* 22
M White Campion 22
S Common Chickweed 24
M Ox-eye Daisy *[many & small]* 36
M/T Sea Kale 60
M Black Nightshade 76
B Bramble 76
S/M Scentless Mayweed 86
M Bladder Campion 92

– if bell shaped

S Snowdrop 10
M White Comfrey 24
M Three-cornered Leek 32

– with flowers in a ball

S White Clover 68

– if cone shaped

M Hedge Bindweed 80

– with clusters of flowers

S/M Shepherd's Purse 12
S Shepherd's Cress 14
S Common Cleavers (Goosegrass) 28
M Ramsons 28
B Hawthorn 28
T Cow Parsley *[flat head]* 38
B Wild Privet 42
T Hogweed *[flat head]* 44
M Yarrow 56
M Hedge Bedstraw 68
M Wild Carrot *[flat head]* 82

– with lipped trumpets

M White Dead-nettle 18
S Eyebright 66

a YELLOWISH GREEN flower could be

– with separate petals

Spindle-tree 32
Traveller's Joy 88

– petals forming a cup

T Wood Spurge 20

– with clusters of flowers

B Red Currant 24
S Black Bryony 34
B Ivy 92

– with lipped trumpets

S Wood Sage 78

– with a flat head

T Alexanders 30
M Wild Parsnip 90

a BRIGHT BLUE flower could be

– with separate small petals

S Field Speedwell 14
S Germander Speedwell 48

– with clusters of flowers

M Narrow-leaved Lungwort 12
S Field Forget-Me-Not 16
M Green Alkanet 20
M Bugloss 32

a MAUVISH BLUE flower could be

– with separate petals

M Lesser Periwinkle 12
T Stinking Iris 58

– large head & many small petals

M Field Scabious 58
S Small Scabious 66
S Devilsbit Scabious 86

– if bell shaped

M Bluebell 16
S Harebell 58

– if cone shaped

M Viper's Bugloss *[many small]* 56

– with prickly leaves

M Sea Holly 62

– with clusters of flowers

S Common Sea-lavender 64

– with lipped trumpets

S Ground Ivy 18
S Ivy-leaved Toadflax 28
S Bugle 40
S Self-heal 42
M/T Field Woundwort 72
S Tufted Vetch 74

– with pea shape

S/M Bithynian Vetch 38

a MAUVE flower could be

– with separate petals

S Common Dog Violet 10
M Honesty 26
M Hoary Stock 36
M Cuckoo Flower *[pale]* 48
S/M Bittersweet 80

– if bell shaped

S Clustered Bellflower 54

a PURPLE flower could be

– with separate petals

M Common Mallow 76

– if bell shaped

M/T Common Comfrey 24
T Foxglove 50
S Bell Heather *[tiny bells]* 86

– with clusters of flowers

B Rhododendron *[large]* 36
S Wild Thyme 58
S/M Marjoram 78
S Heather 86

– with pea shape

S Common Vetch 46

– with lipped trumpets

S Green-winged Orchid 28
S Common Spotted Orchid 42
S Early Purple Orchid 46
M Fragrant Orchid 52
S Betony 54
S Pyramidal Orchid 66
M/T Hedge Woundwort 70

– looks like a thistle

M Winter Heliotrope 12
M/T Greater Knapweed 56
M Black Knapweed 68
T Spear Thistle 80
T Lesser Burdock 82, 100
M Saw-wort 84
M/T Creeping Thistle 88

a RED flower could be

M Common Poppy 52
S Scarlet Pimpernel 54

a RED / BROWN flower could be

– with small individual flowers

M/T Houndstongue 46
T Common Figwort 60

MISCELLANEOUS If you cannot find it anywhere else it could be

B Goat Willow (Pussy) 10
S Ribwort Plantain 16
M Lords and Ladies (Wild Arum) 24
M Hoary Plantain 34
T Common Sorrel 44
S/M Sea Purslane 62
S/M Grass-leaved Orache 62
S Salad Burnet 66
T Teasel 82, 100

How astonishingly does the chance of leaving the world
impress a sense of its natural beauties on us.
Like poor Falstaff, though I do not 'babble',
I think of green fields. I muse with the greatest affection
on every flower I have known from my infancy –
their shapes and colours are as new to me
as if I had just created them with a superhuman fancy.
It is because they are connected with the most thoughtless
and happiest moments of our lives.
I have seen foreign flowers in hothouses of the
most beautiful nature, but I do not care a straw for them.
The simple flowers of our Spring are what I want to see again.

John Keats in a letter to a friend, 14 February 1820

The Flowers

What a desolate place a world would be without flowers.
It would be a face without a smile, a feast without a welcome.

C. L. Balfour

1 **Snowdrop** *Galanthus nivalis*

January–March. Small. Damp woods and shady areas. Well established in many lanes, churchyards and cemeteries. There is a wonderful carpet of them in woods near Gladices, Chale Green, and also on the bank in the car park opposite the Griffin public house in Godshill.

2 **Primrose** *Primlua vulgaris*

February–May. Small. The odd flower can be found as early as January. Primroses grow in profusion all over the Island on grassy banks, in woodlands and road verges. My favourite place for Primroses is the banks bordering the road leading to Walter's Copse from Newtown.

3 **Lesser Celandine** *Ranunculus ficaria*

February–May. Small. The flowers are on single stalks. They can be found everywhere in the Spring in woods, hedges and on grassy banks, often in large patches.

They can easily be mistaken for a Meadow Buttercup *(page 28)* or Creeping Buttercup *(page 34)*, although the Buttercup petals are round and the flowers appear much later in the year.

4 **Goat Willow** *Salix caprea*

March–April. Bush. This shrub is often known as Pussy Willow, because of the fluffy stems on which the flowers appear before the leaves. Common in hedges and woodland and damp habitats.

5 **Common Dog Violet** *Viola riviniana*

March–May. Small. In woods and grassy places. Particularly lovely on the chalk downs where large mauve patches can be seen.

6 **Red Dead-nettle** *Lamium purpureum*

Flowers throughout the year. Small. A very common annual, often with purplish aromatic leaves and pale pink flowers.

Snowdrops *acquired a religious significance because their February flowering coincided with Candlemas, the feast of the purification of the Virgin after childbirth, which included scattering white flowers before her image in the candlelight.*

Primrose *means the first flower of Spring, deriving from the Italian* primavera *and French* primeveize *(spring).*

The leaves of the ***Red Dead-nettle****, like those of the common stinging nettle, can be cooked and eaten as a vegetable – rather like spinach. From the days of early Egyptians until quite recently it was used as a fibre for weaving cloth, which was not coarse but fine and strong.*

1
2
4
3
6
5

1 **Winter Heliotrope** *Petasitis fragrans*
November–March. Medium. All over the Island, along the roadside, on footpaths and grassy places you will see the leaves growing in great profusion. Flowers are far less abundant but appear on single stems above the leaves.

2 **Narrow-leaved Lungwort** *Pulmonaria longifolia*
[Local name: blue cowslip or *Good Friday flower]*
April–June. Medium. Once it grew in abundance but it has steadily declined and is now found only in the New Forest, Dorset and the Isle of Wight. On the Island this vivid blue flower can be found between Parkhurst Forest in the West and Rowborough Copse in the East. I have come across it in the northern corner of Parkhurst Forest. It could be confused with Green Alkanet *(page 20)*.

3 **Shepherd's Purse** *Capsella bursa-pastoris*
Grows thoughout the year. Small/Medium. Widespread. A very common weed! Often found on bare or waste ground. Very similar to Shepherd's Cress *(page 14)*, but easily distinguishable by its tiny purse-like seed pods.

4 **Lesser Periwinkle** *Vinca minor*
Late January–May. Medium. Solitary flowers appear in woods and on shady banks, often near ruined buildings. Probably originally a garden escape. Can be found in the north-west corner of Centurion's Copse, in Atkie's Copse, Ningwood, and on St George's Down.

***Periwinkle** is often found in gardens too, as it is a great ground cover! It was brought to this country years ago as a medicinal herb. It is said to be especially good for treating piles, bleeding noses and tooth ache, and herbalists still use it today. There is an old manuscript which says: 'Periwinca powdered with earthworms induces love between husband and wife if they take it first with their food'!*

The binding qualities of periwinkle stems made them ideal for love knots, allegorically binding lovers together: and possibly periwinkle flowers were the origin of 'something blue' for the bride to wear. Periwinkles, like campions, were also called batchelor's buttons because they were used in flirting games.

1
2
3
4

1 **Field Speedwell** *Veronica persica*
Small. Flowers all the year round, though more profusely in late Spring/Summer. Widespread. Often found on bare or waste ground.

2 **Gorse** *Ulex europaeus*
An evergreen shrub (very prickly!). Widespread and flowers all the year round. It grows in hedges and woodland as well as on the downs, where it is very invasive. The lovely deep yellow flowers are particularly special in January when little else is in bloom and they have a wonderful scent of coconut.

3 **Wood Anemone** *Anemone nemorosa*
March–May. Small. The flowers are on single stems and form a carpet. Usually found on clay soil, in ancient woodland and on old hedge banks. They are more frequently found in woods in the North of the Island. There are wonderful carpets in Walter's Copse, Newtown and also in Firestone Copse, near Wootton.

4 **Groundsel** *Senecio vulgaris*
Small. Flowers all the year round. It grows in loose clusters on bare or waste ground and can be found anywhere on the Island. A weed when in the garden!

5 **Dandelion** *Taraxacum officinalis*
[Local name: blowball or *priest's crown]*
Small/Medium. Widespread. I am sure that everyone knows a dandelion! They grow in most grassy places throughout the year, especially in early Summer.

6 **Shepherd's Cress** *Teesdalia nudicaulis*
March–October. Small. Widespread. Grows in open sandy places and on waste ground (is a weed in the garden). Easily confused with Shepherd's Purse *(page 12)*, which is very similar but a larger plant.

In the fourteenth century ***Gorse*** *was a component of the rural economy, grown for fodder and cut for fuel. It is still referred to by some Island farmers as* Vuzz.

Throughout Europe the jagged leaves of the ***Dandelion*** *led to names like* dent-de-lion *(lion's tooth), recalling the champing profile of a heraldic lion. The flowers, picked at the moment when they are coming into bloom, are used in a beauty treatment. One good handful, boiled for half-an-hour in a litre of water, then strained through a fine cloth, gives a toilet water with which the face is washed morning and evening to remove freckles.*

1
2
3
4
5
6

1 **Wild Cherry** *Prunus avium*

[Local name: merry-tree or *merries – the word 'merries' referred to the fruits and is the origin of the name Merrie Gardens near Shanklin].*

Strictly speaking, as this is a tree it should not have been included, but it is a great favourite of mine! The blossom in April is like snow. It occurs in woodland across the Island, especially the south-east. Just past Brook Church at the junction of roads there is a lovely group of trees.

2 **Cowslip** *Primula veris*

April–May. Small. Another Spring favourite. It grows on grassland, cliff tops and the downs – for example, Brook Down and the slopes above St Catherine's Point. But, best of all, take a walk around the moat of Carisbrooke Castle. The cowslips here are wonderful.

3 **Ribwort Plantain** *Plantago lanceolata*

[Local name: soldiers]

April–October. Small. Widespread. Can be found in grassy places, hedgerows and on waste ground.

4 **Field Forget-me-not** *Myosotis arvensis*

April–October. Small. Just a smaller version of its 'garden cousin'. Keep your eyes open and you will find this tiny blue flower growing on wasteland or disturbed ground (set-aside areas in particular).

5 **Field Pansy** *Viola arvensis*

April–October. Small. Flowers on wasteland and disturbed ground. I found them growing amongst weeds on some set-aside land.

6 **Bluebell** *Endymion non-scriptus*

April–May. Medium. Probably one of the most popular Spring flowers! This wonderful mauve/blue flower grows in great profusion on the Island in ancient woods, on hedge banks and on open land, particularly where the soil is sandy and there is no long grass. The bluebells are especially lovely in the woodland area of Mottistone Garden and up onto the downs behind, as well as in Walter's Copse, Newtown and on the north facing slopes of Wroxall and St Boniface Downs.

A popular children's game was to 'shoot' the flowering heads of ***Plantain*** *by wrapping the bendy stems around the neck of the flower head and pulling sharply.*

1
2
3
4
5
6

1 **Greater Stitchwort** *Stellaria holostea*
[Local name: grandad's shirt buttons!]
April–June. Small. A short straggly perennial, which grows in clumps in woods, by the roadside and on hedge banks – in fact, almost everywhere. Its bright white star-like quality lights up the wayside.

2 **White Dead-nettle** *Lamium album*
Medium. The White Dead-nettle is benign. It flowers pretty well all the year round and can be found on hedge banks, roadside verges, and on waste land all over the Island.

3 **Ground Ivy** *Glechoma hederacea*
March–June. Small. A creeping perennial which forms clumps and sometimes great patches of blue. The word 'ivy' is a bit misleading, as it is not really at all like the common ivy and can more easily be mistaken for a patch of violets. It flowers on grassy places, on hedge banks, in woods and particularly on the downs.

4 **Wild Daffodil** *Narcissus pseudonarcissus*
March–April. Medium. One of my favourite flowers. It is smaller than its garden 'cousin' and more delicate. Can be seen in ancient woodland across the Island but with a concentration of sites around Havenstreet. It was formerly seen in hedges and on banks, but is rare in those places today. Please don't pick any – simply look and enjoy.

5 **Catkins of the Hazel Bush** *Corylus avellana*
In January–March catkins can be seen in the hedgerows on the hazel bushes. In the autumn the bushes will be covered with the familiar hazel nut. The wood is used for fencing and basket-making.

6 **Blackthorn** *Prunus spinosa*
[Local name: winter kecksies]
February–May. The flowers of the Blackthorn appear on dark twigs before the bulk of the leaves. Hedges will be white with Blackthorn flowers. If we have an extra cold snap at this time it will be said to be 'a Blackthorn winter'.

The fruit of the Blackthorn is the Sloe *(page 94)*.

1
2
3
4
5
6

1 **Wood Spurge** *Euphorbia amygdaloides*
[Local name: cups and saucers]
April–May. Tall. Flowers in profusion in almost all woody places on the Island and also on the southern cliffs between Luccombe and Binnel Bay. The flowers are easily overlooked as they are green too. (Not advisable to use wild Wood Spurge as 'ground cover' in your garden, as it will soon take over the entire area!)

2 **Wild Strawberry** *Fragaria vesca*
April–July. Small. Flowers on dry grassy land or wooded areas. The fruit is smaller than the cultivated variety, but a delicious flavour when eaten. I found the strawberries ripening by July on a grassy bank on Mottistone Down.

3 **Green Alkanet** *Pentaglottis sempervirens*
April–July. Medium. I don't know why this is known as *green* Alkanet, as the flower is a very bright blue! It usually flowers in large clumps on banks and in wooded areas. Frequently to be found along the Undercliff beween St Catherine's Point and Bonchurch and on the northern slopes of the Downs near Freshwater Bay Golf course, as well as in other scattered localities across the Island.

Could be confused with Narrow-leaved Lungwort *(page 12)* or Bugloss *(page 32)*.

1
2
3

1 **Daisy** *Bellis perennis*
Small. Daisies flower everwhere on short turf all the year round, but more profusely in the summer – especially on lawns!

2 **Musk Storksbill** *Erodium moschatum*
April–September. Small. Flowers on bare and grassy places. It is a creeping plant and forms large patches. I came upon a mass when walking on a footpath at Atherfield. The **Common Storksbill** *(Erodium cicutarium)* is a similar flower but with a smaller seed pod. It is widespread, growing on roadside banks or beside footpaths.

3 **Red Campion** *Silene dioica*
[Local name: tidy robins]
March–November. Medium. Widespread. Flowers are usually bright pink but sometimes paler, having crossed with the **White Campion**. I have found solitary flowers as early as January. By May there are amazingly large patches everywhere, especially on wide roadside verges, hedge banks, and in woods. Drive down into Niton on the road from Blackgang and you will see a wonderful display.

4 **White Campion** *Silene latifolia*
May–October. Medium. Widespread, growing on hedge banks, roadside verges and often more or less bare places. Similar to the **Red Campion**, but stems tend to be more branched and it is not usually found in large patches.
Bladder Campion should be included here, but I didn't get around to painting it until the late summer. *See page 92.*

Chaucer joked that ***Daisy*** *meant 'eye of the day' and claimed it as his favourite flower, growing 'white and rede' in the flowery mead. The Latin name* bellis, *meaning 'war', reflects the plant's value as an instant healing herb on the battlefield.*

Campions *featured often in medieval gardens, providing shades of white and pink, augmented by the deep magenta of rose campion* (Lychnis coronaria). *The latter was introduced from the Holy Land and provided lamp wicks from its furry leaves, hence the name* lychnis, *meaning 'light'.*

1

2

3

4

1 **White Comfrey** *Symphytum orientale*
May–June. Medium. A garden escape. Most frequently found around Ventnor, St Lawrence and Bonchurch, but I saw it by the roadside on the way into Seaview.

2 **Common Comfrey** *Symphytum officinale*
May–June. Medium/Tall. A bushy plant which grows in damp places. Flowers are purple. Widespread, particularly in the eastern Yar valley.

3 **Common Chickweed** *Stellaria media*
A tiny insignificant flower which grows everywhere on bare or cultivated ground throughout the year – a weed in your garden.

4 **Herb Robert** *Geranium robertianum*
April–November. Small. This little bright pink flower is often rather swamped by the leaves, which frequently turn a reddish brown in the autumn. It grows all over the Island on banks and in woods and other shady places.

5 **Red Currant** *Ribes rubrum*
April–May. Bush. Has inconspicuous green flowers in stalked spikes and later, fruit which is probably eaten by birds! Grows in damp woods and hedges right across the Island. I have found plenty in woodland between Shalfleet and Newbridge.

6 **Lords & Ladies** *Arum maculatum*
[Local name: cuckoo babies]
April–May. Medium. The leaves start to appear on hedge banks, woods or shady places in whorls from January. Its tiny flowers are at the bottom of the trumpet and are topped by a finger-like purple spadix which attracts insects for pollination; all are enveloped in the green-hooded spathe. It has a funny smell but insects love it. More conspicuous are the fruits which are bright red and appear from August onwards. *See page 94.*

The well-baked roots of ***Lords & Ladies*** *were once made into a kind of sago, known as Portland Sago, as it was mostly made around the Isle of Portland. The juice from the roots was sometimes used as starch.*

2
3
1
4
5
6

1 **Honesty** *Lunaria annua*
April–June. Medium. Probably orginally a garden escape, but now grows wild especially along the roadside towards St Lawrence and around Niton Undercliff. The dried seed pods can provide attractive decoration in the winter.

2 **Few-leaved Hawkweed** *Hieracium murorum*
May–September. Medium. Flowers everywhere in grassy places, especially later in the summer. *See* Leafy Hawkweed *(page 68).*

3 **Black Meddick** *Medicago lupulina*
April–October. Small. Low prostate annual which grows on bare or grassy ground – very often on the lawn! A 'cousin' of Hop Trefoil *(page 90).*

4 **Red Valerian** *Centranthus ruber*
[Local name: Ventnor pride!]
May–September. Medium. Common and widely dispersed. The flowers are a bright *pink* and appear on walls, rocks, chalk quarries and cliffs. It was a garden plant in the seventeenth century but was already becoming naturalised. It is especially prolific around Ventnor and can be seen in swathes on the chalky banks beside the Military Road approaching Freshwater Bay as well as opposite the Viewpoint Car Park above Blackgang.

***Valerian** was supposed to inspire love and was therefore employed as a love philtre, for it was believed that if a girl wore valerian she would never lack lovers.*

1

2

3

4

1 **Ramsons** *Allium ursinum*
[Local name : gypsy onion (wild garlic)]
April–June. Medium. Flowers in great profusion in shady places especially on chalk throughout the Island It smells strongly of garlic! Drive along the B3399 road past Ashengrove or down the B3323 under the bridge into Shorwell and you will be well rewarded; it looks as if it has snowed. Ramsdown Farm near Chillerton is said to have a name deriving from the old English meaning 'hill where wild garlic grows'.

2 **Green-winged Orchid** *Orchis mascula*
April–June. Small/Medium. Flowers on grassland and in woods and scrub. Smells a bit like cats! The green veins are often indistinct.

3 **Ivy-leaved Toadflax** *Cymbalaria muralis*
[Local name: roving jenny or *roving sailor]*
April–November. Small. Widespread. Trails over walls, fences or rocks. Can be seen on the wall by the gate to Mottistone Church. Not at all like Common Toadflax *(page 80).*

4 **Meadow Buttercup** *Ranunculus acris*
April–October. Small/Medium. Widespread. Found in grassland, meadows and road- side verges. The leaves are heavily divided, which distinguishes it from Creeping Buttercup *(page 34).*

5 **Common Cleavers** (Goosegrass) *Galium aparine*
May–September. Small. Widespread. A straggling plant with tiny down-turned prickles on the stems. Clings to animal fur and human clothes with some tenacity! Found on waste ground, hedges banks and cultivated land – a weed in your garden.

6 **Hawthorn** *Crataegus monogyna*
[Local name: hogiles or hogailes]
April–May. A shrub or small tree which is very prominent in our hedgerows all over the Island (grows well in seaside areas). The flowers can be confused with the Blackthorn flowers, but the leaves are very different. By August berries are turning red. *See page 94.*

*The medieval Church gave **Hawthorn** a new symbolism as the crown of thorns with which Christ was tormented and crucified.*
The local word 'hogiles' referred to the haws. The newly emerging foliage used to be nibbled by children as 'bread and cheese'.

1
2
3
4
5
6

1 **Alexanders** *Smyrnium olustratum*

March–June. Tall. Widespread. Already in January the leaves are appearing and by March the tall bright yellowish-green flowers are starting to appear and will be around until June. It grows in considerable quantity on hedge banks and waste ground, especially around the coast, though it has recently spread inland. Could be confused with Hogweed *(page 44)* or Cow Parsley *(page 38)*, though these both have *white* flowers.

2 **Hedgerow Cranesbill** *Geranium pyrenaicum*

Early May–September. Small. Widespread. Flowers in hedgerows, meadows, waste ground and on hedge banks. Sometimes difficult to see if it is in long grass.

3 **Toothwort** *Lathraea squamaria*

March–May. Medium. This rather strange flower is a parasite. Its hosts are hazel as well as other trees and shrubs. Locally it is quite common. Occasionally the flowers could be lemon-yellow or beetroot red. I found it flowering in Eaglehead Copse on the north side of Ashey Down – a particularly good site.

1
2
3

1 **Marsh Marigold** (King Cup) *Caltha palustris*
[Local name: batchelor's buttons]
March–August. Tall. Flowers in damp places, by ponds, marshes or ditches. The flowers are similar to, but larger than, a Buttercup *(see pages 28 and 34)*, but the leaves are quite different. It's not so common these days as land becomes more frequently drained.

2 **Three-cornered Leek** *Allium triquetrum*
April–June. Medium. Flowers on hedge banks, stream banks and other shady places. It could easily be confused with Ramsons *(page 28)*, but does not smell of garlic! The strange name refers to the three-sided stem. I saw a clump growing on the bridleway between Kingston Farm and Dungewood Farm, and also a large clump on the hedgebank at the Nunwell end of Doctors Lane, Brading.

3 **Coltsfoot** *Tussilago farfara*
February–May. Small/Medium. Widespread. Can be found on damp grassland throughout the Spring. The flowers appear well before the leaves. I found a lovely patch growing on the footpath where it leaves the Shanklin & Sandown Golf course and crosses towards Sandown Airport.
Could be confused with a Dandelion *(page 14)*.

4 **Bugloss** *Anchusa arvensis*
April–September. Medium. Still found frequently in arable fields and waste land on sandy or gravelly soils. I saw it in a field by a footpath at Atherfield and also in a field at Brading as late as October. Could be confused with Green Alkanet (*page 20* – check the leaves) or Narrow-leaved Lungwort *(page 12)*.

5 **Spindle-tree** *Euonymus europaeus*
May–June. These insignificant little white flowers are the fore-runner of the bright pink and orange berries of the autumn *(see page 98)*. Frequently found at the edge of woods, in scrub and in hedgerows, mainly in the north of the Island.

*Together with **Dogwood** the wood of the **Spindle-tree** was formerly used to make skewers* (Skivers) *for butchers.*

1
2
3
4
5

1 **Black Bryony** *Tamus communis*
[Local name: wild vine or *murrain berries]*
May–August. Small. Widespread in woods and hedges. Twines itself (clockwise) over hedges, but interestingly has no tendrils. The flowers are in tiny insignificant strings, but the berries are an eye-catching bright red *(see page 94).*
I have found flowers and fruit on the footpath linking Broad Lane and the B3399.

2 **Yellow Rattle** *Rhinanthus minor*
May–September. Small/Medium. Flowers mainly in grassy places and can readily be found on the downs, but uncommon away from chalk. It has an inflated calyx, inside which the seeds rattle when they are ripe.

3 **Creeping Buttercup** *Ranunculus repens*
May–September. Medium. Extremely common and widespread in meadows and on grassland, especially wet clay soils. Also found on roadside verges. The leaves are different from the Meadow Buttercup.

4 **Hoary Plantain** *Plantago media*
May–August. Medium. Widespread. Is a larger version of its 'cousin' the Ribwort Plantain *(page 16)* and similarly grows on chalk grassland, hedge banks and waste ground.

According to Bromfield (1856) ***Black Bryony*** *berries 'steeped in gin, were used as a popular remedy for chilblains, acting as a counter-irritant.'*

Any medieval painting of Christ or the saints that showed grass at their feet also showed ***Plantain****. Its traditional name was waybread and it was believed to grow wherever man's foot trod or, glorified a little, to indicate the passage of sanctified feet; this was certainly the case in Ireland where Plantain was dedicated to St Patrick.*

1
2
3
4

1 **Rhododendron** *Rhododendron ponticum*
May–July. Bush. Originally from Asia, *Rhododendron ponticum* has become naturalised in Britain, Belgium and France. Whilst it can be found in gardens, it can become very invasive. It thrives on acid soil and can be seen on Mottistone Down in close proximity to Brook Hill House, in various woods around Shanklin, Alverstone, and in Appley Woods near Ryde.

2 **Ox-eye Daisy** *Leucanthemum vulgare*
[Local name: horse daisy]
May–September. Medium. Widespread. Can be seen by the roadside, often forming great 'snow-like' swathes. Also in meadows and on grassland generally.

3 **Thrift** *Armeria maritima*
May–August. Small. The flowers are at their peak in late May when they carpet grassy areas along the cliffs, in upper salt marshes and the turf behind sandy shingle. In the West Wight they can be a spectacular sight above Freshwater and Compton Bays and also above the shoreline at Hamstead Ledge. In the East Wight visit St Helens Duver.

4 **Flowering Rush** *Butomus umbellatus*
June–August. Medium. Flowers usually by or near fresh water, but is almost extinct on the Island. I saw a large clump in Wilmingham Lane in 2006, but it disappeared shortly afterwards when the verges were cut and didn't flower there again in 2007.

5 **Hoary Stock** *Matthiola incana*
May–June. Medium. Considered to be a native of the Island. It is confined to the south-facing chalk cliffs between Tennyson Down and Compton Down, the calcareous cliffs between St Catherine's Point and Bonchurch and the inland cliff at West Cliff, Niton. I myself have found largish clumps growing beside the Military Road above Freshwater Bay.

1
2
3
4
5

1 **Cow Parsley** *Anthriscus sylvestris*
[Local name: Queen Anne's lace]
April–early June. Tall. By May the hedges and banks all over the Island are white, decked with this lacy flower. It can easily be confused with Hogweed *(page 44)*, which is much more robust and flowers a little later.

2 **Yellow Iris** *Iris pseudacorus*
June–August. Tall. Well distributed across the Island. This lovely Yellow Iris flowers by fresh water streams and ponds and on marshland. It can be seen at the Freshwater end of the bridlepath (course of the old railway) running between Yarmouth and Freshwater.

3 **Bithynian Vetch** *Vica bithynica*
May–June. Small/Medium. A scrambling plant which is becoming rarer but may be found in grassy places and on banks. It could be confused with Common Vetch *(page 46)*, which has a smaller, more reddish violet flower but also grows in grassy areas.

1
2
3

1 **Herb Bennet** *Geum urbanum*
May–September. Medium. Widespread. This rather small, insignificant flower grows in shady places on banks and especially in woods. Once spotted, you find that you see it all over the place!

2 **Kidney Vetch** *Anthyllis vulneraria*
May–July. Small / Medium. Locally it forms colonies on chalk grassland, especially on disturbed sites, slipping chalk cliffs, old quarries and road cuttings. It can be seen on the disused railway track at Bembridge and on undercliffs along the south coast. I saw carpets of it on the slipping cliffs above Compton Bay.

3 **Bugle** *Ajuga reptans*
April–June. Small. Widespread. Flowers in damp grassy places and woods. Could be confused with Ground Ivy *(page 18)*, but is more erect.

4 **Dogwood** *Cornus sanguinea*
May–July. A deciduous shrub. Widespread. Flowers in great profusion in hedges, and woodland fringes. Although the leaves and flower heads are a different shape it can easily be confused with Wild Privet *(page 42)*, which flowers at the same time. The berries are a rich black in the autumn *(see page 98)*.

***Dogwood** shares the local name of 'skewerwood' with **Spindle-tree** (page 98) as both woods were used to make butchers' skewers.*

1.
2
3
4

1 **Self-heal** *Prunella vulgaris*
June–November. Small. A low, creeping perennial which can form great patches of mauve. Grows on grassland (downs), road verges and hedge banks, and other grassy areas. Very impressive on Brook Down. Could be confused with Betony *(page 54)*.

2 **Wild Privet** *Ligustrum vulgare*
May–August. Bush. A 'cousin' of the Garden Privet but with much smaller leaves. This shrub grows in our hedges in great abundance. It can be easily confused with Dogwood *(page 40)*, but the flower heads are a completely different shape, and the leaves are a different shape too! Wild Privet is still flowering in the hedgerows long after Dogwood has disappeared. See page 98 for the berries.

3 **Greater Birdsfoot Trefoil** *Lotus pedunculatus*
June–August. Medium. Widespread. The flowers are the same shape as its 'cousin' Birdsfoot Trefoil *(page 66)*, but the leaves are broader and it is generally a larger plant. Can be found on damp grassland and marshes.

4 **Common Spotted Orchid** *Dactylorhiza fuchsii*
June–early August. Small/Medium. Widespread. Our commonest orchid, found in woodland, on the downs and roadside verges, but not on sandy soil.

Self-heal *is still used in herbal treatment as a general tonic and as an infusion made up of 1oz of dried herb to 1pt of boiling water. It is also used in a poultice form as a cleansing herb for wounds and to stop bleeding.*

The name ***Orchid*** *came from the Greek word* orchis *(love), and orchids have long been associated with love, the pods being used to brew love potions.*

Orchids *that have brown spots on their leaves were said in the Middle Ages to be marked with the redeeming blood of Christ, and were named Gethsemane or crossflowers, in German* kreuzblumen.

1
2
3
4

The two flowers on this page can be found all over the Island.

1 **Hogweed** *Heracleum sphondylium*
April–October/November. Tall. A big chunky plant that is easily confused with its more delicate 'cousin' Cow Parsley *(page 38)*. You can sometimes find the odd flower as early as January. It grows on hedge banks, roadside verges, and in open woods. See page 100 for the seedheads.

2 **Common Sorrel** *Rumex acetosa*
May–June. Tall. The tiny flowers turn from green to rust and then brown. It can be found throughout the summer growing on grassland and in woods.

The leaves of ***Sorrel*** *can be chewed! They are very tasty, with a vinegar flavour (very popular with us as children!). They can be used in salads to give a sharp flavour.*

Recipe for Sorrel Soup

225g (8oz) sorrel leaves
125g (40z) lettuce or spinach leaves
1 onion
225g (8oz) potatoes

25g (1 oz) butter
1.1 litres (2 pints) stock
salt & pepper
150ml (¼ pt) cream (optional)

Shred the leaves, Chop the onion. Slice the potatoes. Melt the butter in a pan and gently fry the leaves, onion and potatoes. Boil the stock and pour over the vegetables. Simmer for 10-15 minutes. Rub through a sieve and add seasoning. If cream is used stir it in just before serving.

1
2

1 **Early Purple Orchid** *Orchis mascula*
[Local name: kettle cases]
April–June. Small/Medium. Can be seen on our downs and in ancient woods in Spring.

2 **Houndstongue** *Cynoglossum officinale*
May–August. Medium/Tall. The flower is rather insignificant and is often 'swamped' by the downy leaves. It smells of mice! It can be found in two main areas: the West Wight Downs and the Undercliff.

3 **Common Rock-rose** *Helianthemum nummularium*
May–September. Small. This rock-rose has a woody stem and a sprawling habit. It is widespread on south facing chalk grassland, on scrub and on most of our downs. I found it on Mottistone Common and by the side of the Military Road approaching Freshwater Bay. It can also be found between St Catherine's Down and Ventnor. Can easily be confused with Creeping Cinquefoil *(page 72)* or Silverweed *(page 70)*.

4 **Common Vetch** *Vicia sativa*
April–September. Small. Widespread. Flowers throughout the summer on bare or grassy ground, hedge banks and woodland rides.

1
2
3
4

1 **Cuckoo Flower** *Cardamine pratensis*
[Local name: milkmaids]
April–June. Medium. Found in damp woods and meadows. The species is in decline. I have shortened the stem so that I could show how the leaves grow at the base.

2 **Ragged Robin** *Lychnis flos-cuculi*
May–August. Medium. Widespread in damp meadows, woods, marshes and ditches. This species is also in decline.

3 **Germander Speedwell** *Veronica chamaedrys*
March–July. Small. Widespread and common on hedge banks, woods and grassland. I saw a brilliant clump growing on a bank near Brook Church in April.

4 **Common Fumitory** *Fumaria officinalis*
May–October. Small/Medium. Widespread. Found on waste ground and rough places. Often a weed in gardens.

In medieval Europe, the little blue flowers of both ***Forget-me-nots*** *and* ***Speedwells*** *signified remembrance, their interchangeable names being* ne m'oubliez mye *and* vergiz mein nicht. *In tournaments, with their aura of romance, the victor's collar was worked with either of these blue flowers, and the name 'speedwell' may derive from this custom, like another old German name for the plant meaning 'prize of honour'.*

1
2
3
4

Mid-summer now!

1 **Dog Rose** *Rosa canina*
June–July. Bush. The hedges are aglow with wild roses all over the Island. Usually pink but can be almost white. In autumn the hips *(page 98)* are easily recognizable.

2 **Foxglove** *Digitalis purpurea*
June–September. This tall, handsome plant grows singly, but often in spectacularly large groups. Usually found in woodland clearings, hedge banks and heathland. Take the path from Brook Hill House across Mottistone Down and you will see plenty. Alternatively walk on St Catherine's Down in the area of the Hermitage. A children's game used to be popping the unopened flowers.

3 **Elder** *Sambucus nigra*
May–July. Widespread. This shrub with fragrant flowers can be found in woods, hedges and waste places. It could be confused with Dogwood *(page 40)* or Wild Privet *(page 42)*, but the flowers are in a more flat-topped cluster. The flowers, picked fresh, make a delicious cordial, whilst the berries *(page 94)* can be used for Elder Wine.

*In the name **Dog Rose** 'Dog' is a corruption of 'dag' (a dagger) – an allusion to the sharp thorns. These flowers have no honey but are loved by bees for their pollen.*

Recipe for Elderflower Cordial

25 heads of Elderflower
50g (2 oz) citric acid
1.6kg (3½ lbs) granulated sugar
2 lemons
*1.5 litres (2½ pints) **cold** boiled water*

Slice the lemons thinly and put all the ingredients into a bowl/bucket to marinade for two days. Stir now and again. Strain and bottle. The syrup lasts for approximately two weeks in the fridge or it can be frozen. Dilute the syrup with water for a cool, refreshing drink.

1
3
2

1 **Fragrant Orchid** *Gymnadenia conopsea*
June–July. Medium. Like all orchids, it flowers on grassy chalk soil, but is rare on the Island.

2 **Common Poppy** *Papaver rhoeas*
June–October. Medium. A family favourite! The lovely red poppy is widespread. It can be found amongst the corn, along the roadside – in fact on any disturbed ground. Occasionally a newly ploughed field will become a sea of poppies.

3 **Greater Spearwort** *Ranunculus lingua*
June–September. Medium. Grows on wetland and marshes. The flower could easily be confused with the Buttercup *(pages 28 & 34)* or Marsh Marigold *(page 32)*, but its leaves are a completely different shape. It is rare, but grows on the edge of our own naturalised pond.

4 **Red Clover** *Trifolium pratense*
[Local name: broad clover or *cow grass]*
May–September. Small. Widespread. Usually pinkish purple in colour. A clover crop is frequently grown as cattle fodder. If you find a four-leaved clover it is said to bring you luck.

*Our **Poppy** contains no drugs like the opium poppy and the seeds are used extensively in both European and Middle Eastern cookery.*
Poppies like to grow on disturbed ground and that is why they appear on land that has been fought over. As we know, they appeared on the battlefields of Flanders after the First World War and have been adopted as the symbol of remembrance.

Recipe for Red Clover Wine

21 flowers
4.5 litres (4 qts) boiling water
3 lemons
2 oranges
1.8kg (4lbs) granulated sugar
28g (1oz) yeast

Pour boiling water over the flowers and leave until lukewarm. Slice oranges and lemons, add sugar and yeast. Put all together in a bowl and leave for five days, stirring twice a day. Strain, and leave for another five days. Bottle and leave for ten days, leaving corks loose. Finally, cork and leave for at least a month.

1
2
3
4

1 **Field Bindweed** *Convolvulus arvensis*
June–September. Small. Widespread. This pretty pink flower is a 'cousin' of the much larger **Hedge Bindweed** *(page 80)*. It sprawls over grass, climbing up anything to hand, mainly on waste ground or in hedgerows.

2 **Betony** *Stachys officinalis*
June–October. Small. Can be found in ancient woodland rides, on grassland, and hedge banks. On the Island it can be seen on the downs between Brook and the Needles. Could easily be confused with **Self-heal** *(page 42)*, but it is much more purple.

3 **Scarlet Pimpernel** *Anagallis arvensis*
May–October. Small. Widespread. It sprawls over the ground either individually or in a small clump. The flowers open only in sunshine. Grows on sandy soil on waste ground or cultivated land. A pretty weed!

4 **Clustered Bellflower** *Campanula glomerata*
June–October. Small. Grows on grassland individually, not in large clumps. Commonly found in the West Wight on the downs between Calbourne and the Needles. It rarely occurs in the East Wight, except occasionally on Bembridge and Culver Downs.

5 **Yellow-wort** *Blackstonia perfoliata*
June–November. Small. Grows individually on chalk grassland. Widespread on the south facing downs and undercliffs right round the coast as well as the odd quarry – Prospect Quarry at Tapnell and Lacey's Quarry, Totland. In 2007 I saw it in great abundance on the south side of Brook Down.

*In the Middle Ages **Betony** was considered a most powerful healing herb, used in the legendary forty-seven remedies compiled by Caesar's doctor. No physic garden was without its slender, pink-flowered stems, valued far more than mint, thyme or other related plants. Betony is still a herbal tea, and for those mysterious complaints, like migraine, stress and digestive disorders that baffle conventional medicine, it could well, for some, still prove miraculous.*

*The **Pimpernel** is said to have appeared where Christ's blood fell to the ground. The plant was therefore taken as a talisman against witchcraft. Its common name of 'poor man's weather glass' refers to the fact that the flowers do not open in rainy weather, not even when rain is expected.*

1
2
3
4
5

1 **Yellow Horned-poppy** *Glaucium flavum*
June–September. Medium. A very conspicuous flower with its horn-like seed pods. Can be seen on undisturbed shingle beaches and on chalk cliffs. Look out for it on the Military Road, where the chalk cliffs begin above Freshwater Bay, and out on Hamstead Point.

2 **Greater Knapweed** *Centaurea scabiosa*
June–October. Medium / Tall. Widespread. Grows on hedge banks and on grassland, including cliff edges. Similar to Black Knapweed *(page 68)*, but much larger. Could be confused with a Thistle, but it has no prickles!

3 **Viper's Bugloss** *Echium vulgare*
May–September. Medium. This brilliant blue flower appears on dry grassland and other bare places on both chalk and sand. It is particularly lovely on Brook and Compton Downs, in the Rowridge Valley and on banks around Carisbrooke Castle.

4 **Yarrow** *Achillea millefolium*
June–November. Medium. Widespread. Grows on hedge banks and grassy places. It often grows in quite conspicuous clumps on the road verges. It is sometimes pink.

*Over the centuries **Yarrow** has been grown in physic gardens and used for healing the sick in convents. Country people used the bruised herb, or an ointment made from it, for burns and small wounds. Its bitter leaves were once used as a flavouring for beer.*

1
2
3
4

1 **Stinking Iris** *Iris foetidissima*
May–July. Tall. Can be found in woodland, on hedge banks, and rough grassy areas. It is especially abundant on the Undercliff. The flower is sometimes difficult to see because of its dense foliage. The seed heads, which appear from August into the autumn, are a spectacular orange *(see page 96).*

2 **Honeysuckle** *Lonicera periclymenum*
June–October. Bush. A woody climber which twines clockwise over other vegetation. Can be seen scrambling over hedges all over the Island. It is particularly lovely on Headon Hill, Totland, where it contrasts with the heather, with a background of the Solent. And don't miss the lovely scent! See page 98 for the berries.

3 **Field Scabious** *Knautia arvensis*
[Local name: gypsy rose or *Egyptian rose]*
June–October. Medium. Widely dispersed on the downs, hedge banks and roadside verges. With the constant cutting of verges scabious are declining, but at present there are still clumps to be seen in Broad Lane, Thorley.

4 **Harebell** *Campanula rotundifolia*
July–October. Small. One of our most delicate flowers, it can be found on dry grassland and heaths. On the Island it has declined but can still be found on areas such as Brook Down, Headon Warren and Bleak Down.

5 **Wild Thyme** *Thymus polytrichus*
May–September. A tiny prostrate flower, mat-forming and colourful, with woody stems. Can be found on the downs and free-draining coastal grassland along the south-west coast as well as St Helens Duver.

It was once a popular pastime for children to pick the individual ***Honeysuckle*** *'horns' to suck for nectar.*

Scabious *takes its name from the Apothecaries' Latin* scabiosa *meaning a plant for scabs. In the past it was known as the Scab Herb, as its juices were said to cure the scab, the mange and the itch!*

The name ***Thyme*** *derives from a Greek word meaning 'to fumigate', and a type of incense was made from the plant to drive away insects. It was once a favourite for flavouring stews, and the good housewife always kept it handy beside the kitchen fireplace, as thyme keeps its aromatic qualities for years.*

1
2
3
4
5

1 **Common Figwort** *Scrophularia nodosa*
June–September. Tall. Widespread. Found growing near streams, in woodland margins and damp places.

2 **Sea Kale** *Crambe maritima*
June–August. Medium/Tall. A substantial plant which forms big clumps. The flowers are not very conspicuous and are often swamped by the large leaves. It grows on shingle beaches around the coast. I found it on Hamstead Point.

3 **Sea Bindweed** *Calystegia soldanella*
June–September. Medium. Very local on sand dunes and shingle. It can be seen on Norton Spit, St Helens Duver and Bembridge Point.
See also Field Bindweed *(page 54)* and Hedge Bindweed *(page 80)*.

1
2
3

All the plants on this page can be found by the coast.

1 **Sea Holly** *Eryngium maritimum*
June–September. Medium. An extremely prickly plant, growing on sand and shingle, but becoming rare. It can be seen on Norton Spit, Yarmouth.

2 **Rock Samphire** *Crithmum maritimum*
July–October. Medium. A coastal plant commonly growing on rocks and cliffs. Grows abundantly on the south coast. I found plenty on the slipping cliffs at Totland and round to Colwell Bay.

3 **Golden Samphire** *Inula crithmoides*
July–October. Small / Medium. Only found on the Newtown and Medina estuaries. On the Medina it is confined to the northern end below Cowes.

4 **Sea Purslane** *Halimione portulacoides*
July–September. Medium. Common on all salt marshes. I have found it growing abundantly at Newtown.

5 **Grass-leaved Orache** *Atriplex littoralis*
July–October. Medium. Can be found on beaches and estuaries along the north coast, often on muddy soil. I found it at Newtown.

***Rock Samphire** is known as the herb of Jupiter. Its stems used to be eaten raw, pickled or lightly cooked.*

1
2
3
4
5

1 **Meadowsweet** *Filipendula ulmaria*
June–September. Tall. Prefers wet meadows, near streams and other damp places throughout the Island. It is very plentiful on the roadside on the Newport side of Shalfleet traffic lights.

2 **Common Sea-lavender** *Limonium vulgare*
July–September. Small/Medium. Grows on salt marshes on the north coast. A wonderful sight on the marshes beyond Walter's Copse, Newtown in late July–August.

3 **Marsh Mallow** *Althaea officinalis*
August–September. Tall. Can be found on most of our main estuaries, sometimes under the shade of fringing oaks where ancient woodland borders salt marshes. I found it at the edge of Walter's Copse, Newtown.

*The old English name for **Meadowsweet** was Meadwort or Meadsweet as it was used for sweetening the mead, which was formerly a popular alcoholic drink. It is also a useful medicinal herb, which is good for all kidney troubles, rheumatism and infectious diseases. 'Take a few handfuls of fresh cut flowers and soak them in a litre of red wine for several hours – and drink a glass with each meal'!*

*Herbalists appreciated the soothing properties of **Mallow**, and the root was also used to make marsh mallow sweetmeats.*

1
2
3

We walked on Brook Down on 27 July 2007 and it was like a garden.
All the flowers on this page can be seen there (especially after plenty of rain).

1 **Salad Burnet** *Sanguisorba minor*
May–September. Small. Shortish perennial with round heads. It is most conspicuous when the heads turn reddish brown. It is rather an unusual flower but grows in large quantities on the downs and can also be found on Bembridge Point and Hamstead Duver.

2 **Birdsfoot Trefoil** *Lotus corniculatus*
[Local name: Tom Thumb]
May–September. Small. Common and widespread. More or less prostrate perennial with much shorter stems than its 'cousin' Narrow-leaved Birdsfoot Trefoil *(page 84)*. Flowers in grassy places and can form a 'golden mat' on the downs.

3 **Squinancywort** *Asperula cynanchica*
June–September. The smallest flower in this book – with the longest name!
It covers the ground making it look almost as if it had snowed. The flowers are pale pink to white and appear on short, old chalk grassland in exposed situations.
Can be found on the downs as well as St Catherine's Point.

4 **Eyebright** *Euphrasia officinalis*
June–October. Widespread. Another small flower to be found in grassy places, especially on the downs. It is mainly prostrate, but if the grass is long it can be two inches tall.

5 **Common Centaury** *Centaurium erythraea*
June–September. Small/Medium. Widespread on dry grassland, heaths and shingly beaches. I found it growing in huge quantities in a field alongside a footpath leading up from the road onto Headon Warren. Also seen on Mottistone Common, usually in clumps.

6 **Small Scabious** *Scabiosa columbaria*
June–October. Small. Similar to its 'cousin' the Field Scabious *(page 58)* but smaller and with a shorter stem. Grows on the downs in profusion.

7 **Pyramidal Orchid** *Anacamptis pyramidalis*
June–August. Small. Widespread. It grows on chalk grassland, including the downs.

Every county has its own flower and the ***Pyramidal Orchid*** *is the flower of the Isle of Wight.*

1
2
3
4
5
6
7

1 **Leafy Hawkweed** *Hieracium umbellatum*
June–November. Small/Medium. Widespread. Grows in grassy places and on hedge banks. See also Few-leaved Hawkweed *(page 26).*

2 **White Clover** *Trifolium repens*
June–September. Small. Widespread. Can be found on any grassland, meadows, hedge banks. See Red Clover *(page 52).*

3 **Black Knapweed** *Centaurea nigra*
June–September. Medium. Widespread. A similar flower to the Greater Knapweed *(page 56)*but with a much smaller, thistle-like head. Can be seen in any grassy place. Worth walking in the meadows close to Newtown Creek in June. They are aglow with flowers, especially Knapweed.

4 **Hedge Bedstraw** *Galium mollugo*
June–September. Medium. Widespread. A sprawling plant, often in clumps. Grows on hedge banks (Broad Lane) and grassland.

5 **Redshank** *Polygonum persicaria*
June–October. Small. Widespread. A sprawling, low annual which can be found on bare ground, particularly on moist sandy soils and around pond margins.
Note the black spots on the leaves.

6 **Lady's Bedstraw** *Galium verum*
June–September. Medium. Very similar to Hedge Bedstraw *(4 above)*but smaller.
It grows on grassland and hedge banks.

Knapweed *was at one time used as a medicine to treat sores, bruises and even sore throats. It has a number of different names – hardhead, topknots, bottlebrush, chimney sweep – all self-explanatory!*

1
2
3
4
5
6

1 **Agrimony** *Agrimonia eupatoria*
June–September. Medium / Tall. Widespread. Grows in single spikes in dry grassy places, often on lime. I found masses growing by the roadside approaching Newtown Town Hall.

2 **Hedge Woundwort** *Stachys sylvatica*
June–October. Medium / Tall. Widespread. A common plant found on hedge banks, woodland edges and waste ground. Could be confused with Field Woundwort *(page 72).*

3 **Silverweed** *Potentilla anserina*
May–August. Small. Grows in damp, grassy places, edges of ponds and coastal habitats across the Island. The flowers are solitary but the leaves form a dense mat and are quite conspicuous because of their silvery backs. Could be confused with Creeping Cinquefoil *(page 72)*, which has a similar flower but very different leaves, or Common Rock-rose *(page 46).*

1
2
3

1 **Elecampane** *Inula helenium*
[Local name: velvet duck]
June–September. Tall. Originally a garden escape. It is rapidly becoming rare, but can be found in Brading churchyard and also in Broad Lane, close to the Thorley crossroads.

2 **Field Woundwort** *Stachys arvensis*
April–October. Medium / Tall. Originally a cultivated plant. Now found in hedgerows and arable areas, but is generally declining. I have found it in Wilmingham Lane, Thorley. *See also* Hedge Woundwort *(page 70).*

3 **Creeping Cinquefoil** *Potentilla reptans*
June–September. Small. Widespread. Grows on grassland, bare places, road verges and banks. Can be an invasive garden weed! Could be confused with Silverweed *(page 70)* or Common Rock-rose *(page 46),* but has very different leaves.

In plays performed by the mummers, the Doctor used a potion called 'hell-and-come-pain' in his comic and ultimately successful attempt to revive the dead combatants. This potion was ***Elecampane****, named after Helen of Troy (whose powers included healing), and containing a medicinal agent now called helenin.*

1
2
3

1 **St John's Wort** *Hypericum perforatum*
May–September. Tall. Widespread and commonly to be found on grassland, in fields, woods and hedge banks. I saw it in great profusion on Mottistone Down in July. Could be confused with Ragwort *(page 92)*.

2 **Tufted Vetch** *Vicia cracca*
June–August. Small. Particularly in the late summer this brilliant mauve/blue flower can be seen almost anywhere on the Island in woodland, hedgerows and rough grassy places. It often forms large clumps on hedges.

3 **Rest-harrow** *Ononis repens*
[Local name: cammock]
July–September. Small. Widespread, particularly on the chalk downs and other coastal grasslands; sometimes on hedge banks.

In the Middle Ages a festival of midsummer bonfires in June was known as St John's Day when Hypericum was lit because it burned away disease and misfortune. As a result, it was given the name of ***St John's Wort****.*

Rest-harrow *is reputed to communicate its nauseous goat-like odour to the milk and cheese of cows in a pasture where it abounds. Cheese so tainted is said to be 'cammocky'.*

1
2
3

1 **Common Mallow** *Malva sylvestris*
June–October. Medium. Common it is, and widespread! This mallow flowers on waste land, hedge banks, roadsides and cliffs. In 2007 Broad Lane, Thorley was mauve with mallow flowers for most of the summer and probably all over the Island too. A really lovely sight.

2 **Black Nightshade** *Solanum nigrum*
July–September. Medium. Widespread. Found on cultivated ground as well as waste places and rubbish tips.

3 **Bramble** *Rubus fruticosus*
May–November. Bush. Widespread. This is the flower of our delicious wild Blackberry. It can be white or pink. Mainly found in hedgerows, but also grows on the downs. See *page 96* for the fruit.

4 **Common Fleabane** *Pulicaria dysenterica*
July–September. Medium. Likes damp meadows, verges, marshes and woodland. Although widespread it is not often found on dry chalky soil.

Enchanted by the way the edible seeds of ***Mallow*** *are packed into little circular cases, like cheeses, the Dutch called them* keeskens cruyt. *In this country the crunchy green fruits used to be eaten by children and referred to as 'cheeses'.*

Nightshade *is commonly used in herbal remedies. The berries are poisonous.*

The daisy-like flower of ***Fleabane*** *was once burnt to form a cloud of smoke for repelling biting insects.*

1
2
3
4

All the plants on this page were found on Mottistone Common in August.

1 **Rosebay Willowherb** *Chamerion angustifolium*
[Local name: tame withy]
June–August. Tall. A patch-forming plant that grows on open heathland and waste ground. (After the war it covered bombed sites and was known as 'Fireweed'.) Prefers acid soil and woodland clearings. It can be seen in abundance on Headon Warren and Mottistone Common.

2 **Wood Sage** *Teucrium scorodonia*
July–September. Small/Medium. Widespread. Flowers profusely in open woods, rough grass, heathland and hedge banks.

3 **Marjoram** *Origanum vulgare*
July–September. Small/Medium. Widespread on dry grassland. Also found on dry walls and on clay soils by the coast. Useful for culinary purposes. Pleasantly scented.

***Marjoram** was cultivated by the Greeks, who believed that Aphrodite had created it. They called it 'joy of the mountains'. It is a herb which is widely used for culinary purposes.*

Recipe for Marjoram Dumplings

50g (2oz) self-raising flour
25g (1 oz) shredded suet
1 tablespoon fresh finely shredded marjoram leaves
pinch of salt
sufficient cold water to make a dough

Mix all the ingredients together. With floured hands form into small round balls for including in a stew or tiny ones for soup.

2
1
3

1 **Spear Thistle** *Cirsium vulgare*
July–September. Tall. Widespread. Can be found on bare ground and waste places as well as on the downs. It is very prickly!

2 **Common Toadflax** *Linaria vulgaris*
June–October. Medium. Fairly widespread, but declining. Can be found in hedges and on banks, roadside verges and waste ground. It is often in clumps and quite conspicuous.

3 **Hedge Bindweed** (*also known as* Larger Bindweed) *Calystegia sepium*
[Local name: granny pop out of bed]
June–September. Medium. It can be seen scrambling over hedges and bushes in any waste places and woods, often swamping its 'host' plant. It is a dreaded, persistant weed in the garden, though the flowers are attractive in the *wild*!

4 **Bittersweet** *Solanum dulcamara*
May–September. Medium. Widespread. The berries turn green, then yellow and finally red – and are poisonous. Found in woods, scrub, hedges and waste land. Could be confused with Black Nightshade *(page 76).*

*In the fifteenth century **Hedge Bindweed** became known as Convolvulus and regarded as so beautiful that it was allowed to grow over arbours both in the Islamic gardens of Spain and in England.*

The local name 'granny pop out of bed', which was used until recently, referred to the manner in which the seeds could be squeezed out of the capsule.

1
2
3
4

1 **Teasel** *Dipsacus fullonum*
July–August. Tall. Widespread. A conspicuous, prickly plant that grows in bare and sparsely-grassed areas, and waste land. Probably better known for its brown dead stems and flower heads *(see page 100)*, which are around for most of the winter.

2 **Wild Carrot** *Daucus carota*
June–August. Medium. Common and widespread. Found on grassland, roadside verges and around the coast. Could be confused with Cow Parsley *(page 38)*, but is much smaller and flowers later in the year.

3 **Lesser Burdock** *Arctium minus*
July–September. Tall. Widespread. A sizeable plant, though the flower is insignificant. It can be found in shady waste places, hedgerows or woodland clearings. Like the Teasel, it is probably better known for its seed heads *(see page 100)*, which are extremely sticky; the hooked bracts catch on clothes, dogs' fur, etc!

***Burdock** is popularly called 'Dock' on account of its huge leaves, but unlike the true Dock all its parts are not only edible, but wholesome. It is an important medicinal herb. The leaves, made into a poultice, can be applied externally to relieve gouty swellings, bruises or any inflamed surfaces.*

1
2
3

1 **Hemp Agrimony** *Eupatorium cannabinum*
[Local name: raspberries and cream]
July–September. Tall. Widespread. Grows abundantly in hedgerows, roadside verges, woodland, marshes and on undercliffs.

2 **Saw-wort** *Serratula tinctoria*
July–October. Medium. Grows in damp places on the northern side of the Island. Also occurs on the downs at the western end. I found a large patch in Walter's Copse, Newtown. Could be confused with Black Knapweed *(page 68)* or mistaken for a Thistle.

3 **Narrow-leaved Birdsfoot Trefoil** *Lotus glaber*
June–August. Medium. Scarce. Very similar to the Greater Birdsfoot Trefoil *(page 42)* but brighter and with much narrower leaves. Found in rough pastures and coastal areas.

4 **Broad-leaved Willowherb** *Epilobium montanum*
July–September. Medium. Quite different to Rosebay Willowherb *(page 78)* but has similar long seed pods. The tiny pink flowers are dwarfed by the leaves. Can be found in shady waste places and woodland. A widespread weed!

5 **Wild Mignonette** *Reseda lutea*
June–September. Medium. Conspicuous because it forms a clump. Flowers mostly on chalk. I found it growing in the chalk pit on the Military Road as it rises above Compton Farm heading towards Freshwater Bay.

1
2
3
4
5

1 **Bell Heather** *Erica cinerea*
July–September. Small. Found on open heathland and dry heath woodland. The main sites for both Bell Heather and Heather are Headon Hill and Ventnor Down. These two plants bloom together and provide a brilliant contrast to the background of blue sea. The name Headon Hill derives from the Old English words meaning 'the hill or down where heather grows.'

Recently the scrub on Mottistone Common has been cleared and Bell Heather planted. It is now spreading rapidly and is worth seeing in August.

2 **Heather** *Calluna vulgaris*
July–September. Small. Whilst not quite such a bright mauve as Bell Heather it is nonetheless attractive and has the same habitat.

3 **Devilsbit Scabious** *Succisa pratensis*
June–September. Small. Grows in damp, grassy places. I found it in Firestone Copse, near Wootton.

4 **Scentless Mayweed** *Matricaria perforata*
April–November. Small/Medium. Semi-prostrate annual, which flowers throughout the Island on bare ground and waste land (areas of 'set aside').

5 **Smooth Sow-thistle** *Sonchus oleraceus*
May–November. Medium. Grows on waste or disturbed ground everywhere. Sometimes known as Field Thistle. Could be confused with the Prickly Sow Thistle *(page 88)*.

1
2
3
4
5

1 **Traveller's Joy** *Clematis vitalba*
July–September. Widespread. This wild clematis is often known as **Old Man's Beard** because of the woolly seedheads which cover our hedges in the autumn *(see page 96).* A clambering woody perennial which grows particularly on chalk and limy clay. The small green flowers are fragrant and can be swamped by the large leaves.

2 **Creeping Thistle** *Cirsium arvense*
June–September. Medium/Tall. Common everywhere on grassy verges, meadows and waste ground.

3 **Prickly Sow-thistle** *Sonchus asper*
June–September. Medium. Common on bare soil and waste ground everywhere. Sometimes known as Spiny Milk Thistle. Could be confused with the **Smooth Sow-thistle** *(page 86).*

4 **Musk Mallow** *Malva moschata*
July–August. Medium. Although quite widespread, it is ususally a solitary plant. It grows on roadside verges and grassland including the downs, but rarely on the coast. I found a large clump on Brook Down in August.

*Some older Island countrymen remember smoking cigar lengths of the dried stems of **Traveller's Joy** when they were 'nippers'.*

***Musk Mallow** was formerly used in the preparation of herbal cough medicines. It takes its name from the musk-like smell of the leaves when crushed.*

1
2
3
4

1 **Great Willowherb** *Epilobium hirsutum*
July–September. Tall. Often forms great clumps. Prefers an open, sunny spot in damp and waste places, ditches and pond margins. I have found it in Broad Lane, Thorley where the Hamstead Trail crosses the road.

2 **Wild Parsnip** *Pastinaca sativa*
July–September. Medium. Grows on grassland, banks, waste places and dry soil. Particularly abundant on chalk. Has a strong smell. I have found it in Broad Lane, Thorley opposite the quarry. Could be confused with Alexanders *(page 30)*, but that flowers in the early summer and the Wild Parsnip does not appear until later and is smaller.

3 **Hop Trefoil** *Trifolium campestre*
May–September. Medium. Widespread. Similar to Black Meddick *(page 26)* but much bigger. Grows in grassy places everywhere, especially on chalky or sandy soil.

4 **Wild Basil** *Clinopodium vulgare*
July–September. Medium. Widespread in open woodland, hedgerows and dry grassland.

1
2
3
4

1 **Bladder Campion** *Silene vulgaris*
[Local name: bull rattles]
May–September. Medium. Widespread. Found on roadside verges, waste ground and edges of arable fields, but never in quantity. Note the inflated sepal-tube, which forms a 'bladder' – hence the name. I should have painted this earlier in the summer as it flowers abundantly in May/June. However, it continues to be around until late September. See page 22 for the Red and White Campions.

2 **Ragwort** *Senecio jacobae*
June–November. Medium/Tall. Widespread. Grows in dry grassy places, overgrazed fields and on rough ground. It can be very invasive and is poisonous to cattle – the farmers' enemy!

3 **Rough Hawkbit** *Leontodon hispidus*
June–October. Small/Medium. Grows on chalk grassland and dry waste places. The Lesser Hawkbit is similar but has a shorter stem; it flowers abundantly on the downs towards the end of the summer. Could be confused with Dandelion *(page 14)* or Hawkweeds *(pages 26 & 68)*.

4 **Ivy** *Hedera helix*
September–November. Bush. Widespread. Grows in woodland and hedgerows and on walls and old buildings, often in dense shade.

1
2
3
4

Now reaching the autumn, the following three pages are devoted to a few of the berries which dominate our landscape from September through to November.

1 **Lords and Ladies** *Arum maculatum*
[Local name: cuckoo-babies]
These bright berries can be seen on hedge banks by early September (if not in late August). The leaves, so predominant in the Spring, seem to have disappeared.
See page 24 for the flower.

2 **Elder** *Sambucus nigra*
By late August the Elder bushes are black with ripe berries. Time now for Elderberry Wine. Twigs were used by children to make whistle pipes.
See page 50 for the flower.

3 **Sloe** (Blackthorn) *Prunus spinosa*
[Local name: winter kecksies]
By late September/October the Blackthorn bushes will be laden with the bluish black Sloes. Time now for Sloe Gin *(see below)*.
See page 18 for the Blackthorn flower.

4 **Hawthorn** *Crataegus monogyna*
[Local name: hogiles or hogailes]
The crimson berry of the Hawthorn dominates our hedgerows from August onwards. A feast for the birds but not for humans.
See page 28 for the flower.

5 **Black Bryony** *Tamus communis*
[Local name: wild vine]
I don't know why it is called Black Bryony, as the berries are bright red! The insignificant little flower *(page 34)* has now become a major player in our autumn hedgerows as it twists and turns over the bushes.

Recipe for Sloe Gin

Sloes
Gin
Barley sugar
Almond essence

Half fill clean, dry wine bottles with the fruit previously pricked with a darning needle. Add to every 28g (1 oz) crushed barley sugar 2-3 drops of almond essence. Fill the bottles with unsweetened gin, cork securely, and allow to remain in a modestly warm place for three months. Then strain the liquor through fine muslin or filter paper until quite clear. Bottle, cork securely and store for use.

1
2
3
4
5

1 **Guelder-rose** *Viburnum opulus*
This bunch of brilliant red berries is a spectacular sight in the autumn. I found it in Wilmingham Lane, Thorley. The leaves too turn a wonderful deep red before they fall. Frequent in ancient woodland and old hedgerows on the clay soil of the north side of the Island. Rare in the south.

2 **Bramble** (Blackberry) *Rubus fruticosus*
A fruit that is commonly picked in the autumn. Bramble jelly is delicious.
See page 76 for the flower.

3 **Traveller's Joy** (Old Man's Beard) *Clematis vitalba*
The small green flower *(page 88)* has turned into a cloud of fluffy seedheads which dominate our hedgerows well into the late autumn/winter.

Gerard, the herbalist, says: 'A plant decking and adorning waies and hedges where people travell and thereupon I have named it Travellers' Joie.'

4 **Stinking Iris** *Iris foetidissima*
The seedhead full of bright orange berries lights up the hedgebanks, woods and rough grassland in the autumn.
See page 58 for the flower.

Recipe for Blackberry & Apple Jelly

1.8 kg (4lb) blackberries
1.8 kg (4lb) cooking apples
1.1 litres (2 pts) water
sugar

Rinse the fruit. Cut up the apples without peeling or coring. Simmer the blackberries and apples separately with the water for about an hour, until the fruits are tender. Mash well and allow to drip through a jelly bag. Measure the juice. Bring to the boil, then stir in the sugar (usually 450g/1lb to each 600ml/1pt of juice). Boil briskly till set.

1
2
3
4

1 **Dogwood** *Cornus sanguinea*
[Local name: skewerwood]
Very much part of the autumn hedgerow. Can easily be confused with **Wild Privet** *(below)*, as both have black berries. The shape of the heads and leaves are quite different.
See page 40 for the flower.

2 **Wild Privet** *Ligustrum vulgare*
The **Wild Privet** berries linger on long after those of the **Dogwood**. More food for the birds! See page 42 for the flower.

3 **Spindle-tree** *Euonymus europaeus*
[Local name: stinkwood or *skiverwood]*
Has a small, insignificant flower *(page 32)*, but the **Spindle-tree** comes into its own in the autumn with brightly coloured fruit and leaves that change through gold to a deep red.

4 **Honeysuckle** *Lonicera periclymenum*
The pretty flowers are followed in the autumn by red succulent berries.
See page 58 for the flower

5 **Dog Rose** *Rosa canina*
Similarly, the flowers give way in autumn to bright red hips, which are a favourite with birds. The hips can be used to make Rose Hip Syrup *(see below)*. In the war years children were given it to supplement their diets. See page 50 for the flower.

Recipe for Rose Hip Syrup

3.3 litres (6 pts) water
1.4 kg (3 lb) ripe, wild, rose hips
900g (2 lb) preserving sugar

Boil 2.2 litres (4 pts) water. Mince the hips coarsely and put immediately into the boiling water. Heat until water boils again, skim off the scum as it rises and boil for a few minutes. Then allow to cool for about 15 minutes. Pass the pulp through fine linen or muslin twice to ensure that all the hairs are removed. Put the liquid obtained to one side. Boil the pulp again with the remaining 1.1 litre (2 pts) water, leave to cool for 15 minutes and strain twice as before. Return both extracted liquids to the pan and boil until the juice is reduced to about 1.7 litres (3 pts). Sweeten, stirring well. Pour into warmed bottles and seal. Store in a dark cupboard until needed.

1
2
3
4
5

And finally, three seedheads which dominate our hedgerows at the turn of the year.

1 **Teasel** *Dipsacus fullonum*
See page 82 for the Teasel in flower.

2 **Hogweed** *Heracleum sphondylium*
See page 44 for the flower heads.

3 **Lesser Burdock** *Arctium minus*
See page 82 for Lesser Burdock in flower.

***Teasels** sprayed with gold make pretty Christmas decorations.*

1
2
3

My Favourite Walks for Flowers

Walter's Copse, Newtown
for Primroses, Bluebells and Wood Anenomes. Also Firestone Copse.

Mottistone Common (and Mottistone Manor)
for Bluebells, Foxgloves and Pink Campion. Also Ventnor and Wroxall Downs.

Hamstead Ledge
for Thrift, Sea Kale and Yellow Horned-poppy. Also the cliffs between Freshwater and Compton Bays.

Brook Down, Wellow Down and Afton Down
for summer grassland flowers.

Newtown Estuary
Walk through Walter's Copse to the estuary for a fine display of Sea-lavender.

Headon Warren
for Heather, Bell Heather and Rosebay Willowherb. Also Ventnor Down.

As a starting point for planning walks of all lengths and all over the Island you cannot do better than visit the website: www.catbells.streamlinenettrial.co.uk. All the walks are beautifully annotated and fully illustrated with photographs taken *en route.* There is also a definitive map showing all the Island's rights of way with their reference codes.

I urge you to go out and enjoy our wonderful wild flowers, but please just *look* rather than pick! And definitely don't uproot any !

Index